Change Y
Thinking Pattern and
Attitude

Your Personal Guide
to Positive Behavior
Change

Brian Azarenka

Copyright

© 2013 Brian Azarenka

ISBN: 978-1-304-09923-5

Terms of Use

Any information provided in this book is through the author's interpretation. The author has done strenuous work to reassure the accuracy of this subject. If you wish you attempt any of the practices provided in this book, you are doing so with your own responsibility. The author will not be held accountable for any misinterpretations or misrepresentations of the information provided here.

All information provided is done so with every effort to represent the subject, but does not guarantee that your life will change. The author shall not be held liable for any direct or indirect damages that result from reading this book.

Contents

Introduction

It's expected that one of the hardest aspects of life is having the ability to persevere.

Words can only state what you can or will do, but actions make those words a reality.

Now, before you start, you have to know that this book is written to help you shape up your old habits. This is not a book that will compliment every aspect of your personality.

This book will help you only if you will allow it to help you. That means, in order for you to see results, you have to be willing to strive for results.

The whole point of you reading this book is for you to be able to change your attitude afterwards was it not?

You're sick and tired of having to deal with your old habits. You don't want to look at others and envy them for what you lack.

You want to develop a new and better habit for you to live with everyday. That is what this book will help you do.

It will help you change your outlook and attitude in life. Your old negative feelings will be gone, replaced by the new and positive attitude that you have gained.

Yet, you won't be able to reach your goal without effort. It's going to require a lot of effort in the beginning. However, the more you believe, the more you'll achieve. Keep up the good work and keep going no matter what.

You have to remember, changes are permanent only if you continue those changes. It can be very easy and tempting at times to change back to your old self.

The reason why it can be difficult for you to change yourself is because you are too comfortable.

People enjoy their comfort zone. They do not like the idea of it being popped, broken, shattered, trespassed, or whichever term people tend to phrase it as.

The point is, once their comfort zone is broken, there's a very high chance of them moving back into the zone after a certain period of time.

It's like forming a new habit. Normally, it'll take at least three weeks for a new habit to form, that's if you continued the same routine for that long.

Likewise, forming a new habit is the same as breaking away from your comfort zone because in order to change something, you must first rid yourself of what you've had before.

It's good to put yourself on the spot sometimes when you are trying to change yourself up. The more you look at what you haven't done and what you could've done, the easier it will be for you to strive for the change that you want.

Although motivation is key to absolute success, motivation only lasts outside of the comfort zone. If you continue to stop letting yourself be too comfortable where you're at, you're doing something right.

Granted, chances won't appear in a few days. It's going to take weeks, or maybe even months. Either way, the more you keep going, the closer you'll be to your goal.

That's the purpose of this book: to help you reach that goal. You want to change your attitude about life? Do it. Don't waver and don't procrastinate.

Whatever amount of time that you're going to take to read this book, take in every minute and every word.

Don't think that you're wasting time. You're spending time shaping yourself up. That's what's important.

In this book, you're going to run into some parts that will make you feel uncomfortable just by reading about it.

It's going to make you angry and it's going to make you question yourself. The point is to suck it all up and learn from it.

Change is all about being uncomfortable. If you're too comfortable then you're not changing. Take every word in and make it count. Don't waste your time if you aren't willing because time isn't going to sit around and let you waste it.

Chapter 1: The Reality

Life is harsh and will forever be harsh. Reality is a part of life that no one wishes to look at. Granted, most people tend to simply run away and constantly escape to their fantasies, hoping that luck will eventually play its way into their lives.

However, there are the few who tend to stay within reality's point of view. Even so, what is their actual reality?

Most people have different viewpoints as to how life works or how a life should be lived. That viewpoint will often shape their reality. It's the same for you.

Do you see life as being simple or harsh? There are probably about 80% of people out there who believes that life is very hard and that stability is the only way to live.

Nonetheless, there are the other possible 20% who states that life is easy and enjoys every moment of it. Now that doesn't mean that those with simple believes do have it easy.

Rather, it can be quite the opposite. A rich man can clearly state how easy life can be through the results of his efforts while a poor man can clearly state how difficult life can be through the efforts of his complaints.

If you didn't catch the meaning behind those words, it means that the more you complain about what you need to do, the harder it will be to accomplish it.

Likewise, the more time you spend on accomplishing your goals, the easier it'll be for those efforts to bloom over time.

You can't dawdle around and complain in life, expecting that you will achieve something in the process. The only way to do something is to stop talking and do it.

Hard work pays off and so does patience and shaping up that negatively unmotivated attitude is the foundation of future success.

The Need for Motivation:

In life, there will always be something that goes wrong. Whether it is caused by you or by someone else or through time, life will find ways to push you down after you've gotten back up.

That's how reality is and that's how life works. Of course, that type of pressure will affect everyone the first few times. However, humans adapt. That's how we are and that's the instincts that we are born with.

We are an adaptive type of species. We will change overtime as we are constantly looking for a change in ourselves.

So why is it that some people cannot adjust to life's negative pressure? It's because they cannot adapt.

Some people choose to stay still and accept the fact that the pressure will not allow them to move. Others will choose to rebel and adapt to that pressure. That is called motivation.

Motivation is what gives you the ability to continue through life, ignoring the hardships and reaching for success.

If you let life push you around, you will not get anywhere. You will not achieve anything. Most of all, you will spend your nights thinking about what you could have done that you've never bothered to do.

Sure, it may seem nothing at first but as life moves on, you will only be able to see it when it is too late.

Time is ticking in a forward motion. Before you can move along with time, you have to first learn how to move on your own.

Before you can fully motivate yourself into a change, you need to first have a wake-up call. If you feel the need to have life smack you across the face with reality then have it do so.

Life is not fantasy. You cannot imaging and expect. The only way you can succeed in life is if you dream and do. You can't do anything without first doing something.

You've probably heard this saying plenty of times before, "Be realistic." Everyone has heard that.

Everyone that has had goals and dreams and aspirations has heard that. The biggest problem is that the majority of the time, people take it in.

They allow those two basic words to crush their possible future within two seconds. Then they allow life to blind them away from realism.

Ask yourself this, "How do you 'Be realistic'?" If you're thinking about the fact that you have to go to school, graduate college with an impacted degree, get a steady job and a steady income in order to feed your family, then that's not being realistic.

That's being average. You know why that's considered average? It's because almost everybody lives that way. When you're being realistic, you're being innovative.

Do you think you're being realistic by being nobody? You're being realistic when you choose to live for yourself and not through the expectations of others.

Did you think that the inventor of the telephone was "Being realistic" when he wanted to come up with the idea of long distance communication through an object?

What about the Wright Brothers? Did you think that they were "Being realistic" when they came up with the dream of being able to fly?

No, they weren't. They were being realistic by knowing that their goal will be reality and their goal is the reality now. Yet, how were the both of them able to accomplish their goal?

They had motivation. They had the passion to prove people wrong. They had the perseverance to keep going despite countless failures and criticisms from the very people who have recorded their names in the history book.

So now, how do you feel about hearing the words "Be realistic?"

We'll focus more about reality in the next section but, for now, it's about motivation. Think about what you want.

Do you know that majority of people do not know what they want in life?

It doesn't matter how smart they are or whether they have high ranked college degrees. What matters is if they know how to spend the rest of their lives the way that they want to.

Many people don't end up with that answer and it's rare to find those who do. Even as people age, the answer is still left empty and blank.

What does that tell you? Do you want to be those people?

Do you want to spend the next ten, twenty, or even thirty years living a life for a purpose that you're unsure of? Of course you don't.

You want to know exactly what you want. You want to be able to stand on the place that you want to be at. So how would you be able to get there?

Simple, you get there through motivation. If you want something then you have to motivate yourself to go out there and get it. Life isn't going to let you sit back and give you what you want.

Life doesn't spoil you and the people around you aren't going to put up with that lazy attitude of yours when you can't even stand on your own two feet like they can.

If you've got two good pair of legs then why don't you use them? Even people on wheels are moving farther than you are. How does that make you feel?

Hopefully, this will get you thinking about a few things in your life. It's important that you motivate yourself to strive for what you want.

When starting a new goal, don't think about how long with going to take for you to get there. Think about how badly you want to get there. Think about why you want to go there in the first place.

Distance isn't going to help you reach anything. It's about determination and motivation. If you want it then you'll be motivated to do it. Of course, it's going to take time. It's going to take a lot of efforts but it will be worth it.

The key to motivation is to take baby steps. Sooner or later, when time passes by, those baby steps are going to turn into leaps and those leaps are going to take you to your goal.

That is why motivation is important because, if you quit, it's going to be a lot harder to get back on track.

Facing Reality:

If you're reading this book, you're most likely a middle class type of person. You're probably living off paycheck to paycheck with a little extra money here and there.

You have a family to support, or not. You feel that it's hard for you to get by and you want it to change.

This is probably a good estimate. It doesn't mean that every reader has this type of thinking so if it doesn't apply to you then don't worry about it. However, you should apply these next few points in your mind.

The point of this book is to help you change your attitude about life. Most likely, you've had a negative outlook on life and you want to change that.

Well, the big question is how are you looking at life? How are you facing reality, if you're even facing it directly at all? An example would be the cold and honest truth like this one:

A few years after you're born, you're expected to attend school for the first seventeen years of your life.

You'll go through changes. You'll meet new people whether you'll end up liking them or not. You'll go through family arguments and any extra stuff that you want to add in for those seventeen years.

Now, after those seventeen years is when your life actually begins. So basically, for the first seventeen years of your life, your efforts were as equivalent as to a baby taking his/her first steps.

Despite all your previous awards, achievements, and reputations, you are still the baby of society. Then, you grow into college and college becomes the first stage of your adulthood.

It's when you finally start aging because it's going to be the time when people are going to start taking you seriously.

You're now old enough to handle your own responsibilities and pay for your own roof over your head and your own food on the kitchen table.

What's more, you're on your way to the future that you want. You're studying the major that will decide what you will be in the future.

Afterwards, you're going to go out into the world, find a job that you like (or not), take it, and make an income for yourself. That's basically the cycle of life for just about anybody.

Now why would something like that be the truth? It's simple. Think about it for a second. You go to school to get an education in order to find a good and stable job for yourself, correct?

That's the philosophy behind it. Now, here's the harsh reality minus the philosophy. You pay thousands of dollars for an education that will get you a job in order to pay off the debt that brought you to that job. Sounds pretty depressing doesn't it?

Many people won't actually realize it until you point it out to them straight on but, when you do know, don't deny it so easily. Learn to accept the obvious and move on.

So now that you know this, how is it going to change you? Truthfully, it's going to do something.

Although you may not realize it now, it's starting something. You're starting to take a good look at what you've been building on. However, don't be a pessimist about it.

The reason why it's good to take it negativity at an early stage is because you can grow immune to it later on. Negativity is like a disease for people and positivity is the cure.

Let the negativity suck its way into your mind, accept it, and get over it. It may sounds harsh but it's true.

If no one is going to be completely honest with you early on then the pain is only going to extend because you weren't prepared for the worst.

When you're facing reality head on, you are making the first step towards changing yourself. You're prepared and you're ready. You won't allow yourself to fall from something small, even if you've scraped yourself in the process.

That is why know what's in front of you is so important. It's the one key to getting you on track.

Knowing Your Limits:

At a certain point in life, everyone is going to want to dream. They are going to have dreams and they will want to make those dreams a reality. That is the first step to success.

Yet, as people age, they will slowly lose that dream. Some will make a new one and some will abandon it completely.

In the end, it's all up to you. Nonetheless, what are you asking yourself? Are you going to accept what you've done in life and stop caring?

Hopefully not because you've just lost all the years that you've worked for in your life. All those dreams, aspirations, and goals went straight down the drain just because you couldn't bring yourself to continue them.

Think about why you've given up. Was it because it was too difficult or did you just lose the motivation to continue? Either way, that's something for you to answer on your own.

This section isn't all going to be about why you've lost your way. That's just the introductory part.

This section is about you knowing your limits. Sometimes, when people do tend to give up on their goals, it's mainly due to the fact that there is too much work involved.

Now, no one likes work and no one wants to go through with it. That's understandable. However, that shouldn't be a factor in giving up.

Sure, you're going to hit a plateau with all that work and all that effort, but everyone does. Who cares? The most important idea to remember is that you have to keep going.

You can't move at a steady pace. You have to change that attitude of yours of wanting to move constant. You don't want consistency. You want improvement and you want change.

You want to see the graph of your life move up, not down and not across. Before you start to give up, ask yourself how badly you want to reach your goals.

Do you want the results? Will it be worth it? Don't think about the negatives but the positives. That is how your motivation grows. That is how you keep going.

Now, this section is about limits. Continuing from the top, do you know your limits? Most people give up due to work because they don't. They just want to rush and finish as quickly as they can.

Well, in life, you can't do that. The point of a goal is that it's going to take a long time to reach it and a certain amount of effort is going to be required in order to you to reach it.

That's the way life works, but that doesn't mean that you have to make it difficult on yourself. You need to take it slow and plan your schedule out.

Know what you can do within a day and what you can do the next day. Remember, baby steps are important. Without it, you wouldn't be able to walk properly.

Also, this isn't just about what you can do, it's about how far can you go with it. You have to know your limits. You have to know what you can do.

This doesn't mean that you shouldn't push yourself to strive better. It means that you shouldn't do something that is realistically impossible.

Basically, if your goal was to swim at least 50 meters for training, you're not going to magically walk on water with your bare feet. Always try to improve yourself and never limit your actions to the words of those around you.

There are going to be people that will bring you down and it is your job, and your own improvement, to prove them wrong. Never think about what you can't do, but what you can do.

Don't Wait:

This is actually, or should be the number two rule of life itself: don't wait. Waiting are for those with too much time on their hands. When you're waiting, you're losing the time that you could've spent on something else, or someone else.

Don't ever let the spur of the moment stop you from moving. Waiting is the reason why many people feel as if life is moving too slow.

They grow bored and they wait for the moment to end so they can figure out what to do next. Don't do that. Always keep yourself busy no matter what.

Life is plentiful. You can do anything and everything. You have an important meeting to review on in the morning, but you're stuck waiting for the bus at the bus stop?

Get out a piece of paper and start reading. Study while you're waiting. Call someone up if you're bored. Do something.

You want to change yourself then change. What are you waiting for? Who are you waiting for? Life will not change you by the amount of time that you spend doing nothing.

Life will not allow you to change if you stand still and expect it to happen. Life will change you if you are willing to move forward on your own. Life will give you the opportunities to change if you are willing to accept those opportunities.

Life is not an escalator for you to ride on. It is a staircase that you have to walk on with your own two feet.

No one will carry you up there and there will be those who will drag you down. In the end, what do you want?

Do you want to be the one who reaches the top of the stairs first or do you want to be the ones that always try but can never win?

Accept and Move on:

Dealing with different types of people is going to be your biggest challenge in life. Everyone is different. People act differently and speak differently.

You're going to find many people that you don't like, many people that you do like, and very few people that you want to have in your life.

That's the basic theory of human interaction. You're not expected to like everyone and everyone is not expected to like you.

However, common courtesy and respect is still very important so keep that in mind. Just because you don't like the person doesn't mean that you have to offend them.

Likewise, if someone offends you, you don't have to make a comeback. Granted, no one likes to lose in an argument but what is more important to you: time or winning a pointless argument?

You're also going to meet people that will definitely pass on their negative vibes to you. People are going to try to push you down to prove to you that they're better.

They will hurt you, mentally or physically, and they will try to break you. It's all part of life. Everyone will go through with it. What matters is all about how you take it in.

Nowadays, most people are very conscious about what others think of them. Then there are those who don't bother to care completely. Both are the wrong approach.

Granted, they can't help it since it's a personality trait but that doesn't mean that you can't change it.

You want to be conscious but only to a point and you definitely want to ignore it but only to an extent.

It's good to take some negativity in from others every once in a while, assuming that it's good criticism.

Basically, you have to know whom you should listen to and who to not listen to. Self-improvement does rely on others and not just yourself. If you can't see what you need to change then let others see for you.

That's just something for you to keep in mind. Other than that, move on with your life and focus on what matters to you. There is no point in suffocating yourself inside a bubble of negativity. Just pop it and move on.

Chapter 2: Improving Yourself

No matter who or what gets in your way, the biggest obstacle in life is your personal self. The reason why is because no one can make the decision of how you act.

They can dictate but that doesn't mean that you have to go through with it. Your boss at work can command you around but that doesn't mean you have to listen to him.

Nevertheless, you do anyways because you want to keep your job and you need a paycheck at the end of the month. You are making a decision every minute of your life. You choose between doing something and doing nothing.

No one can control your absolute decision. It's your life and therefore, it's your choice to choose how you want to live it.

Society is stressful and many people still do have the habit of blaming others for their misfortune. It's all a part of growing up and, unfortunately, not many people grow up that quickly.

You have to realize that whatever mistake that happens, it's not anyone else's fault but yours. If it was at a bad timing then fine, sure. However, you need to realize that the majority of the time, it's you.

This is crucially important if you have the intention of trying to change yourself. Before you can even think about changing your attitude, you have to first learn how to take responsibility for your own actions.

If you keep pushing the blame on to others, you're not going to know what it is that you need to work on in order to improve yourself.

Control Your Ego and Pride:

Without a doubt, a person's ego is one of the biggest problems about life. People with huge egos tend to, let's say, screw themselves over in the future.

They also tend to irritate those around them. If you've ever been around someone with a huge ego then you should know how he or she is.

Unfortunately, many people with huge egos tend to not realize it until someone points it out for them. Even then, they would ultimately defend themselves with all they've got. These are the hardest type of people to change because they won't easily listen to just about anybody.

They think that they are perfectly fine where they are they will only find people that will like them and put up with them. Later on in life, you'll learn that people with huge egos won't make it very far in society.

A lot of times, people tend to group ego with pride. The two terms are pretty similar nowadays thanks to the people who's made it that way.

Anyways, having an ego isn't bad. Being an egotistical person can be a downfall depending on whom you're with. In the end, your ego is just one aspect that allows you to love yourself for who you are.

Of course, you have to love yourself in order to want a change. When you love yourself, you want the best for yourself. That means the people that you're surrounded by, your environment, your community, and your health.

Yet, don't let yourself become too prideful. You can't think that you're better than someone else even if you may be.

Note that there are those who are better than you and there will be times when you will have to drop that pride of yours. It doesn't make you less of a person if you do.

In fact, it shows a mature side of you that others can come to respect. Many people tend to cling onto their pride thinking that letting go might belittle them. It's actually just doing the opposite in the other person's point of view.

A bit of advice, if you want to better improve yourself, it's best to learn how to control your ego and your pride. It'll do you wonders in the future for both your personality and your life.

An Imitation but Still Different:

Let's put this out: originality is overrated. Nowadays, everybody is trying to be original. They want to be seen as a person who's never copied from anybody.

They want to stand out and, sometimes, they will do some stupid stuff to prove it. In the end, no one is original.

We are different, but we are also the same. The reason as to why we are the same is because when we were born, we were empty. Our personality at the start of our birth is like a blank piece of white paper.

We have nothing to show and we have nothing to act upon. Yet, as we grow older, we start to see the world with our own eyes. We meet new people. We travel to new places.

Overtime, that blank piece of white paper becomes filled up with vibrant colors, each with its own unique set of shades.

That is what makes us similar to everyone else. We take in what we've seen and experience in life. Everywhere we go, every body that we've met, we have allowed them to influence us.

Some may take up more room on our piece of paper while others will only be an obscure little splash of paint, covered by another shade of color. Either way, our personality is mainly developed from others and not ourselves.

At the same time, we are different. Not everyone will be painted the exact same way, which is the reason for our individuality.

It's not exactly originality because there's a slightly different concept of each term. Individuality focuses mainly on yourself and the type of person you stand for. It's what you've made of yourself out of your environment that others can't copy.

Your flaws and your positive aspect are slightly different from someone else. No two people are the same and individuality proves that point.

This is why you should never put yourself down just because you aren't like someone else. If you want to improve yourself, you need to learn how to break away from others.

You need to understand that you are different and that it's good to be different. Chances are you wouldn't want someone to be exactly like you. Do you really think that it'll be good to be exactly like someone?

Do you want to have their personality and all of their flaws? Is being a duplicate of another person really how you want to live your life?

Mostly likely not, right? You want to be yourself. You want to be another person. What is the point of being an individual if you're not going to separate yourself from a clone?

In order to grow, you need to accept everything about yourself. Granted, people are going to drag you down with them, but you can't please everybody.

Know that not everyone will like you. That is the cold, harsh reality. Focus on yourself and on those who deserves your attention. Don't ever belittle yourself.

There are many people out there that constantly drag themselves down because of some little, insignificant phrase that someone has told them.

That is why many people are pessimistic about their life. You need to learn how to take it and let go of that. Don't sulk about it.

If you know that it's true, take it in and improve yourself. If you know that they are wrong about you then ignore if.

If they don't know you then they don't have the right to criticize when the information hasn't been presented to them.

Know that you are going to make mistakes and you are going to do some pretty embarrassing things throughout the course of your lifetime. Make it fun.

Be happy while doing those things. Learn from your mistakes and let it teach you how to grow. The more you try to reject what's in front of you, the harder it'll be for you to accept the truth.

There is nothing for you to be afraid of when you're trying to accept yourself. Remember, change comes after acceptance.

Start changing the way you think because that's what's going to help you change your attitude.

Start Fresh:

It's always good to start a completely new day. Most people tend to carry the weight on their shoulders to the next day. That's fine too if you want to get crushed by it in the future.

Usually, that's called stress. How stress works is that it builds over time. You won't feel it right away in the beginning but it's going to get there some day and, once it does, you're going to feel bad.

Stress can damage you both physically and mentally so you have to be careful. That's why it's good to start off the day completely stress free.

Not only that but you also have a lot of relief on your body. There's nothing for you to worry about and you're able to focus on your work without distractions.

It's especially helpful during the development process since it gives you a bit of release from your past.

It's not going to erase everything that you've done in life but it's going to help make you feel better. You always want to refresh your life at a certain point, hopefully everyday if you can.

It's not good to hang onto something that's already been done and over with. Just move on with the present and work towards the future. It's going to be hard to let go but you can't move on if you don't leave something behind.

Stop Giving Up:

There is no benefit to giving up. You will never meet anyone in the world who has stated that he/she has given up and still be successful afterwards.

It's impossible to achieve something if you're not going to do something about it. That's like saying you want to climb a tree but you're not willing to even touch it.

What you're doing is giving up before you even start and that's a trait that you need to get rid of.

This ties in with procrastination. Don't put things off. If you want something done then do it. Don't make excuses. Don't say that you can do it tomorrow. No, you have today so why wait.

If you can do it today then why should you wait until tomorrow? The longer you put off something, the harder it'll be for you to start it.

You want that big promotion that you've been waiting on for years now?

Well go out there and earn it. Work hard so your boss will believe that you deserve it.

No one is stopping you but yourself. All those negative thoughts that you have should be burned and thrown away a long time ago. If you continue to believe that you can't do it then, for sure, you cannot do it.

It's about time for you to stop waiting on other people. Your friends aren't going to be there to push you every step of the way.

They have their own life and future to live for. Your family is the same thing. They've had their life and now they want a break. Understand that you're no longer a child.

You don't need someone next to you to hold onto your hand. If you want to lead others then lead yourself first.

If you're envious of seeing others achieve what you can't then it's about time you start achieving something for yourself.

Stop telling yourself that there's always next time when you fail. There isn't a next time.

If you fail with an attitude like that, what makes you think that you're not going to fail next time with that exact attitude?

Get the phrase "next time" out of your vocabulary. There isn't a next time, but a "now". If you want to start something then start now and continue it.

Don't start then give up. If you do then you've just wasted your precious time. Start and keep going.

Remember, winners never quit and losers can never win.

Be Specific:

In order to succeed, you need to be specific. Sure, motivation and perseverance plays a crucial role, but how are you going to reach your goal if you don't know where to go?

Making a starting point is as easy as claiming an ending point. What you want to picture in your head is the route between point A and point B because that route is going to give you what you want.

You say that you want to change yourself. How are you going to do it?

Did you know that people who plan out their goals would most likely achieve it than those who just state it?

That's because they know what they want and they know how to do it. It's like when you travel to a new place. You might want to go to a new restaurant that you've heard about from your friends or family. That's great but how are you going to get there?

You're not going to go inside of your car and immediately drive away to an unknown destination. The best plan would be to look up the directions before heading out.

Goals work the same way. Change works the same way.

You want to ask yourself how you're going to accomplish your goal. What are you going to do to change yourself?

Ask yourself simple questions like these and answer them. After that, record your answers and turn them into a plan. Once you've got your plan, put them into actions.

Take Responsibility:

Have you ever heard the phrase, "Take responsibility for your actions"? Well, this is more of an upgrade: take responsibility of your life.

As mentioned before, you live your own life and no one else's. No one is going to live for you. You're a human not a puppet. Don't let anyone control the way you live.

At the same time, do take responsibility for the words that you've said and the actions that you've done. Don't ever push your mistakes onto others.

If you keep using people as an excuse of your flaws then you definitely need a wake up call. Everyone has flaws. If there's a positive side then there's a negative side. You're not perfect and you're definitely not anywhere near it if you can't accept yourself.

If you messed up then you messed up. Accept it, learn it, and move on from it.

Stay Away From Perfection:

Perfection is an aspect that is craved but can never be obtained. Everybody wants it but no one can have it.

With that in mind, it's always good to do the best you can. Use the skills that you've picked up over time and use the knowledge that you've gained throughout the years. Even if perfection is unreachable, that doesn't mean that you can't come close to it.

Perfection should be avoided when you group it together with work. A worker with the mentality of being a perfectionist will become a workaholic.

That's because they're always willing to add more work to their schedule until they've perfected what they want done.

Although being a hard worker is a good mentality to keep in mind, being a workaholic is just one step towards destruction.

If you know anyone who is a workaholic, you would know that they are always working. They have no free time for themselves and they are built up with stress on a daily basis.

Workaholic tends to feel differently than how others may view them. There are many people who respect those with a high work ethic and would, of course, want to be like them.

Through a workaholic's point of view, it is a curse. They would rather take a vacation for a few days then to have to sit down and work every minute of their life.

They continue to work hard because they're conscious of their results. They have very low self-esteem and they will feel as if they did a bad job if it doesn't seem perfect through their eyes.

Don't try to lower yourself into this position. It can be very difficult to grow out of. Although these are the few people who do bother to take action, they're going in the wrong direction.

Truth is, most workaholic doesn't know what they want in life and they work hard in order to make up for that indecisiveness. They mainly see life as a battleground where they have to constantly compete with others in order to maintain their own rank.

This is why it's best if you stay away from being a workaholic and a perfectionist. If you want to improve yourself then this isn't one way of doing it. This is why knowing yourself is so important.

Know what you want and figure out how you're going to get there. If you keep living your life as a workaholic, you can be recognized for the hardest worker but also as one with the least amount of personal progress.

Immerse With Others:

Immerse yourself with other people. There's apparently a new trend nowadays where people tend to stay away from each other or simply dislike one another.

It's fine to dislike someone because the both of you don't get along, but it's a different story when you're trying to completely isolate yourself from reality.

Humans are affectionate creatures. We need others to be around us and we need to be around others.

Now there are introverts who actually live off of being away from people. However, they don't live their life alone. Even introverts need to be around someone. Although the numbers may seem less than those who are extroverts, there is more than one party involved.

In reality, human development does rely on human interaction. Some people won't admit to that but they know it's true.

Even though it's called "self-improvement", you need others to help you improve yourself. You need to take in bits and bits of their personality and habits in order for you change.

That's basically called influence and you can't be influenced if there's no one around to influence you.

Yet, technically, you don't necessarily have to get to know the person to be influenced by them but it helps. Human interaction is very powerful and useful throughout the course of your life.

You can't stay independent as long as you're living. You may feel as if you're independent at certain times but you will never be able to be fully independent.

People are always relying on one another. There's always a small percentage of dependency among people. That is how we work.

You can't be the type of person that shelters your own life away from the outside world. You should know by now that reality will be difficult, mainly because of people.

However, reality will also be fun and worthwhile mainly because of people. In the end, it all boils down to whom you are around throughout the course of your life.

Always try to have a companion in your life. Don't ever let them easily break off the friendship that's difficult to build up. Nowadays, people tend to distrust one another and maintaining a stable connection with one person is difficult.

Yet, once the connection has been set, there's nothing for you to worry about. It's a benefit for you to have trustworthy people around you.

Let them be your support and let them help shape you into the person that you want to be.

There are many types of different relationships that you can have with other people. Friends, family, and lovers aren't the only relationship that's possible.

There are also business relationships, mentor relationships, and common interest relationships. It's good to immerse yourself in many different types of relationship with people.

Having a business relationship with someone will usually include your co-workers. It's more of a professional relationship but that doesn't mean that it can't be a close one.

There have been many cases where co-workers have ended up being a best friend and an important impact in one's life. Besides, having a good business relationship with someone can provide you a useful connection when you need it the most.

They can also help you with work if they were your co-workers. Business oriented people know what to do for a business and can be a tremendous help for you.

The other type of relationship is a mentor-student relationship. Back in school, have you ever gotten along with your teachers? It doesn't have to be all of them or the majority of them.

Even one single teacher is fine. How did it feel to you when you've made a bond with that teacher? Normally, most people will think that it's weird but, in a sense, there's nothing wrong with it.

You have to understand that teachers are also people. They have a job just like anyone else and their job is to teach. Outside their line of work, they are just regular individuals with their own lives.

Those bonds that you've made with them, it doesn't have to be a friendship bond. It's a bond that you've made because you admire them. It's because they have already achieved something that you still lack.

They are your mentors, teachers, and friend. They are there to help you and guide you. You cannot go through life without making a mentor-student relationship.

You will always have someone who is better than you and, likewise, you will always have someone who will be willing to teach you.

However, you should choose carefully. Like all relationship, it can be bad. If you don't choose a proper teacher, then you won't be able to have a proper education with them.

Having a common interest relationship with someone can be very fun. Let's say you want to go to the gym to work out because it's your New Year resolution just like everyone else's.

Well, it's your first day and you're practically alone because you don't have a companion with you. Usually, it's always best to train with someone because they're able to push you past your limit, especially during a good workout.

Now, let's say that you met someone new while you were working out in the gym and, surprisingly, you got along with that person very easily. What you've just developed was a common interest relationship with someone.

This type of relationship can only be established if the other party does share the same mindset as you. You both have the same goal even if the road there is slightly different. This is the type of relationship where the both of you are each other's pillars.

Learn to Listen:

Listening can be one of the hardest things for most people to do. People are genuinely heavy talkers. They want to be the center of attention.

They've got stories to tell and experiences to share. Most of the time, people don't remember what they hear from others. It's more like they don't bother to listen in the first place.

That is a bad habit for you to keep up. Ironically, everybody wants a listener but no one is willing to listen. That doesn't make any sense at all right?

If you want someone to listen to what you have to say then you have to do the same for him or her. Not only is it common courtesy, but also respectful.

You also don't want to interrupt someone when they are talking. That's the exact same thing as being rude.

In a conversation, it's not just about getting your point across to the other person. It's about listening to what they have to say in order for you to have a proper conversation with them.

If you've ever watched a debate, you've noticed how the other party tends to wait until his opponent has finished speaking before he starts to state his point.

Both parties are going to be on the defensive no matter what because they want their side to win.

Either way, they're going to be respectable enough to wait for their turn. It's actually required that they do that. Adults are patient but children bicker.

Also, the same applies for speaking. Do let others talk in a conversation. That's the whole point of the conversation, to converse between two people. If you're the only one doing the talking then you might as well talk to a brick wall.

Of course, you can't particularly control that habit. Most people love to talk and they won't know when to stop because they just have too many topics to talk about.

Yet, when they do stop talking, they usually end up thinking about the next topic that they want to say. Thus, they have ultimately disregarded everything that the other party has said.

It's going to take a while to improve your listening habits but if you keep trying, you'll find that it's quite useful to have.

Besides, you'll notice that other people have many interesting stories to tell. If you don't listen then you can miss out on a lot.

Make Your Own Choices:

This is the last tip: make your own choices. Remember, it's your life to live. People have their own lives to live so you don't need to let them control yours.

Obtain your own independence. Have you ever heard the phrase, "The biggest enemy is yourself"? It's true. The biggest enemy is you. Since you're the only one who can finalize your own decision, you're the only one who is capable of being your number one enemy.

People have two ways to think, one with your heart and the other with your mind. Both ways conflict with each other because your decisions are either going to be moved by your feelings or by your logic.

However, it's always good to give both sides a chance to act. There's always going to be a consequence for everything that you do whether it'll be good or bad so why both letting someone make the decision for you?

You're no longer a little kid. You're an adult and there's no way an adult would let another adult control their life.

If you want to change then you have to take action for that change. Remember, you're the one making the decision to change.

Chapter 3: Be Appreciative

This is going to be heavily emphasized because it's important to take note of. You need to learn how to appreciate life for what you have.

Granted, you're going to feel envious and jealous of things that others do have but that's normal. However, that doesn't mean that you shouldn't appreciate the things that you do have.

One of the biggest mistakes that most people make is that they don't realize how fortunate they are.

If you have a roof over your head, food on the table, and a paycheck to bring home then you are more fortunate than half of the people living on this planet.

Usually, many people often feel depressed about their life because they can't see the fortunes that they have.

They want what they don't have and stop caring once they have it. Many people can easily push what they already have to the back of their mind and disregard it for another object.

Yet, once it's gone, they feel depressed about losing it and by then, it's already too late.

There are even cases where people cannot appreciate themselves. That's similar to having a low self-esteem. Usually, for people who cannot learn to appreciate themselves, they're on the brink of destruction.

They can't see what it is that they have that can make others envy. Everyone has a particular trait that others will like and look up to. No one is that much of a failure.

It all comes down to how you express yourself. If you think that you have nothing worthwhile for people to respect then find it, or obtain it. It all starts by wanting a change.

When you're appreciative of what you have, you're happy. Envy and jealousy can destroy your mental state. It can become a goal for you to obtain something that you don't have, but too much greed can destroy a person.

If you want to change yourself then you have to at least take careful consideration of what you have at the moment. After all, what can you change if you don't know what to change?

Usually, people who are unappreciative end up as a pessimist, something that you want to avoid.

Happiness plays a lot in change also. In order to be completely happy, you must appreciate. If you know that you're blessed then there shouldn't be a reason for you to feel depressed.

Not only can happiness improve your health, it can also give you a push to your goal. You can't expect to change if you continue to be a pessimist.

You're going to have to change that pessimistic side of yours before you can expect to change anything else.

Also, never use death as an excuse. The reason why this is mentioned at the end is because it's the most important. Nowadays, the suicide rate has reached up to about 70% or more.

The stress that society has among people is astonishing depressing. Nowadays, many people view happiness as more of a goal than an actual road.

In reality, you can be as happy as you want. You can be happy anytime you want. If you want to be happy then you will be happy. If you believe that you're sad then you're going to be sad. It's common sense.

Don't ever take your life for granted because you are too tired to live. Believe this, everybody is tired to live. Everyone has their days when they wake up and want to give up.

Yet, they don't and why is that? It is simply because they know that what they're about to leave behind is worth more than themselves.

It is not just obligation, but responsibility. Dying is easy. Anyone can do that. However, living is hard and not very many people can do that. The only problem that society has is the fact that too many people are dying for all the wrong reasons.

Think about it, when you die it's all over. Right now, you want to change. If you're dead then nothing will change. Your problems aren't going to fade away at the foot of your coffin. It's going to stay and it's going to affect the people around you.

If you want to change then continue to live and see your own results with your own eyes. If life wants to drag you down and beat you to your deathbed then you can smack life across the face.

This is why happiness is so important. Every motivating factor that allows you to continue to aim for a particular goal is due to happiness.

Although you may not realize it in the beginning, it's a fact that you should know. Again, appreciate what you have. If you don't, whatever that you've worked for will be pointless.

Conclusion

Now that you've reached the end of the book, how do you feel? It might've been a lot for you to read but, at the end, you've learned something.

Changing isn't easy and it's going to take you a while until you're able to see the results of your efforts.

The best method is to be patient with your progress. Self-improvement does not happen overnight. Work at it everyday and soon, you'll develop a habit that will become an aspect of yourself.

As an overview before you go, remember to always look at life from multiple perspectives. Just your opinion won't do. You need to look at life through the eyes of others before you can grasp a slight understanding of reality.

Do know your limits and what you're capable of doing. Don't state an impossible goal that you know you can't do.

That will only disappoint you in the long run. Sure, going the extra mile is a stretch but only if you're pushing yourself towards someone reachable through your efforts.

Also, don't wait for anyone. If you want to accomplish something then do it. Don't wait for someone's permission.

Don't wait for them to tell you that you should do it. There will be people that will try to drag you down and brush their negativity onto you.

Ignore them and move on. Prove them wrong by doing what you want. If you continue to take other's opinion into consideration then you will go nowhere.

Progress is made through your own efforts and not through the words of others.

Remember, you are a unique individual with your own set of aspects. It's perfectly fine to envy others for their capabilities but only if you can accept yourself first.

You need to realize your own potential before you can learn from others. After all, you can't start as a student if you don't know who should be your teacher.

This is why you should be specific with what you want. It can be very confusing to pursue a goal when you don't even have a clear sense of which direction you're going.

Likewise, it can be difficult for you to try to change yourself if you aren't sure of how to do it.

Just saying that you want to shape up and change isn't going to do anything for you. All you're doing then is stating what you want and not what you will do.

If you want something then you will go after it with full determination.

Stick with people no matter what. Humans are intimate creatures. No matter how much of an introvert they may be, they will need some form of human interaction.

Remember the different types of relationships that were talked about in the previous section. You can pick any one you want.

Keep in mind that relationships are developed naturally and not forcefully. It's not going to work out if you try to act as if you desperately need a friend. By then the other party will start to repel you.

Lastly, learn how to make your own choices. It's your life and it's your choice. There's no reason as to why you should let someone else control your decision.

Don't be the person that requires a hand. Be the person who is capable of lending a hand.

You're not going to be able to change on your own so why wait for someone to help you with it?

You're no longer a child so it's about time to grow up. Listen to yourself before listening to others.

Your needs comes first as well as your happiness.

Hopefully, by now you've gotten at least motivated to change. If you do then keep it up.

Plan it out. Write it out. Then, bring it to action. If necessary, keep a record of your progress and your daily activities. As long as you're doing something that's different from your normal schedule, you are making some form of change.

Don't forget, in order to make a change on your own, you need to be able to step out of your comfort zone and stay out of it.

Printed in Great Britain
by Amazon

54675852R00037